KIDDIES WRITING BOOK

LETTERS, WORDS AND FUN PHRASES

THIS BOOK BELONGS TO

_____

UPPERCASE HANDWRITING PRACTICE

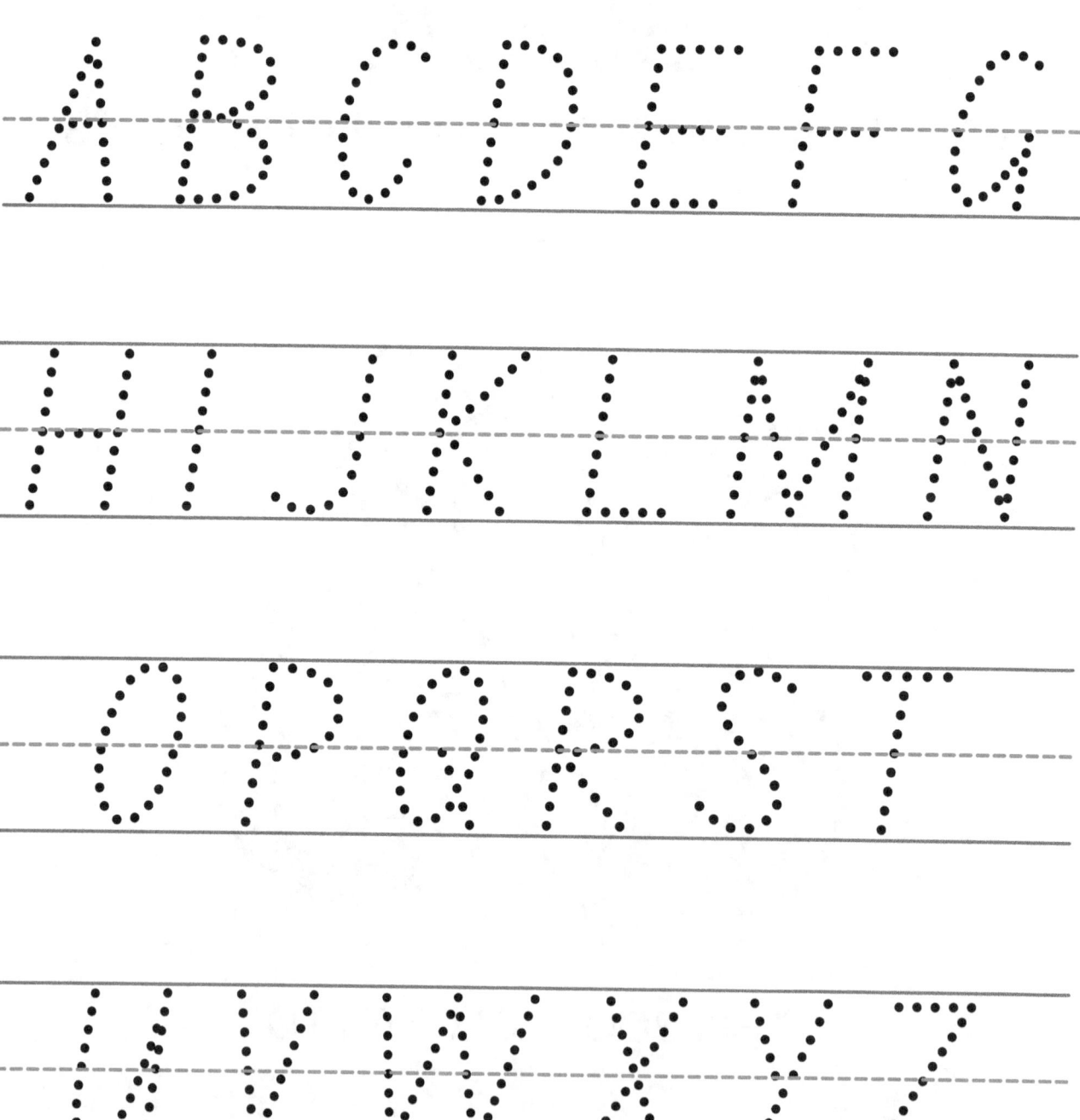

Lowercase Handwriting Practice

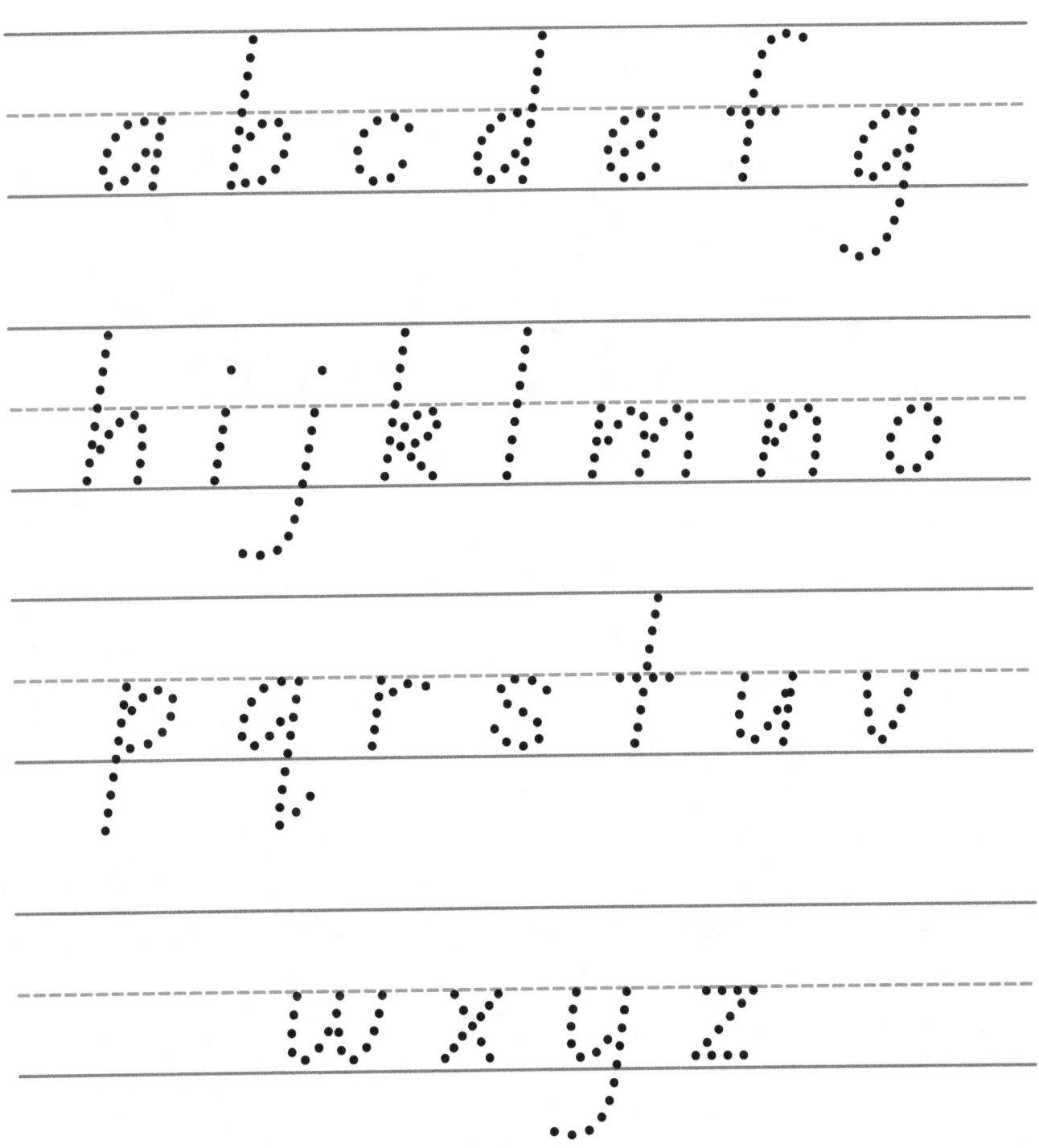

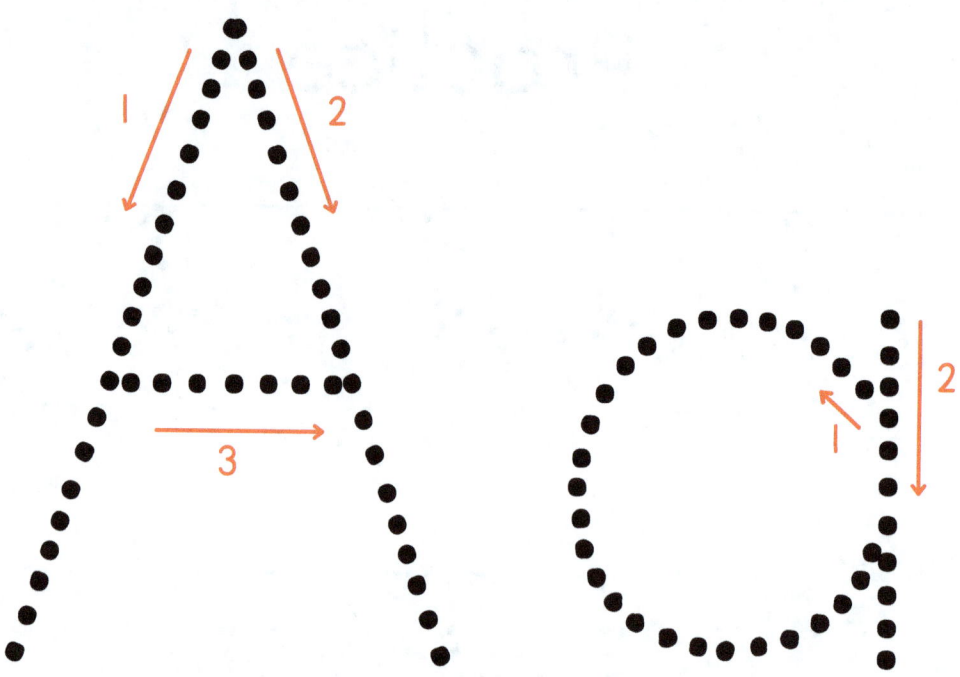

A

a

A

a

Aa Aa Aa Aa

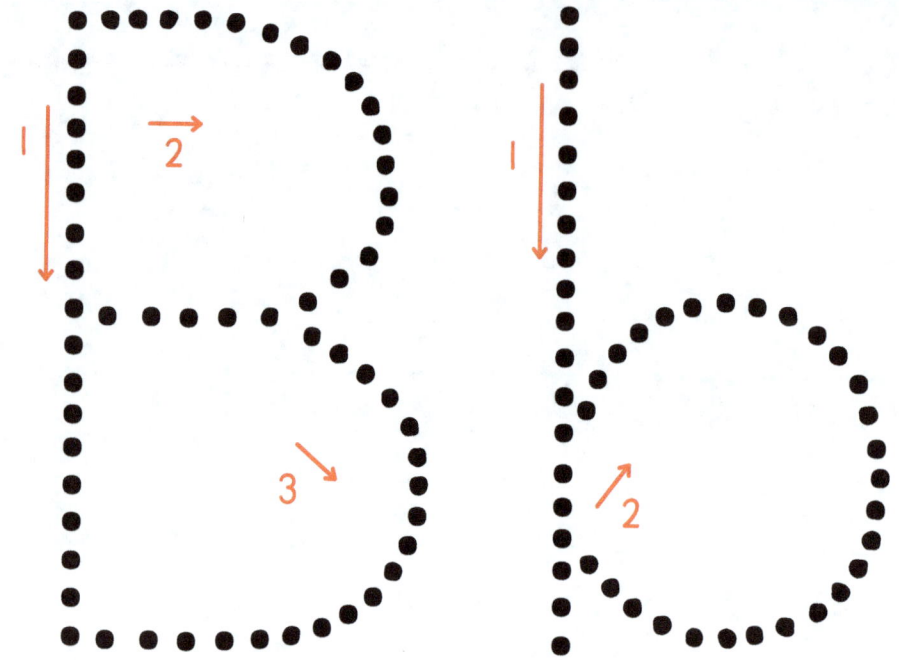

B

b

B

b

B b b B b B b B b

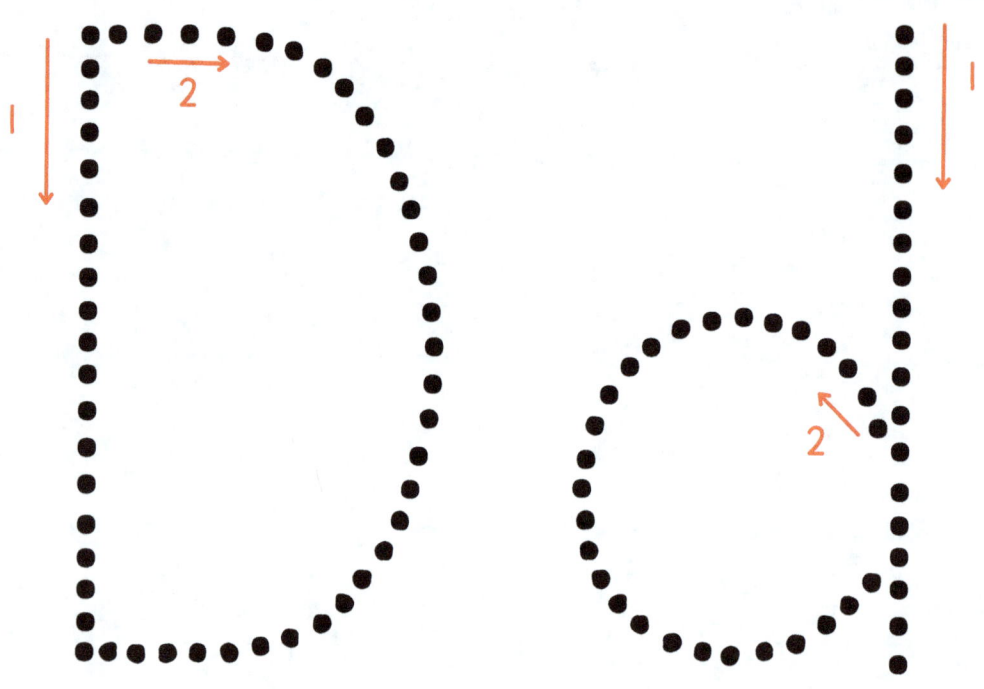

D

d

D

d

D d D d D d D d

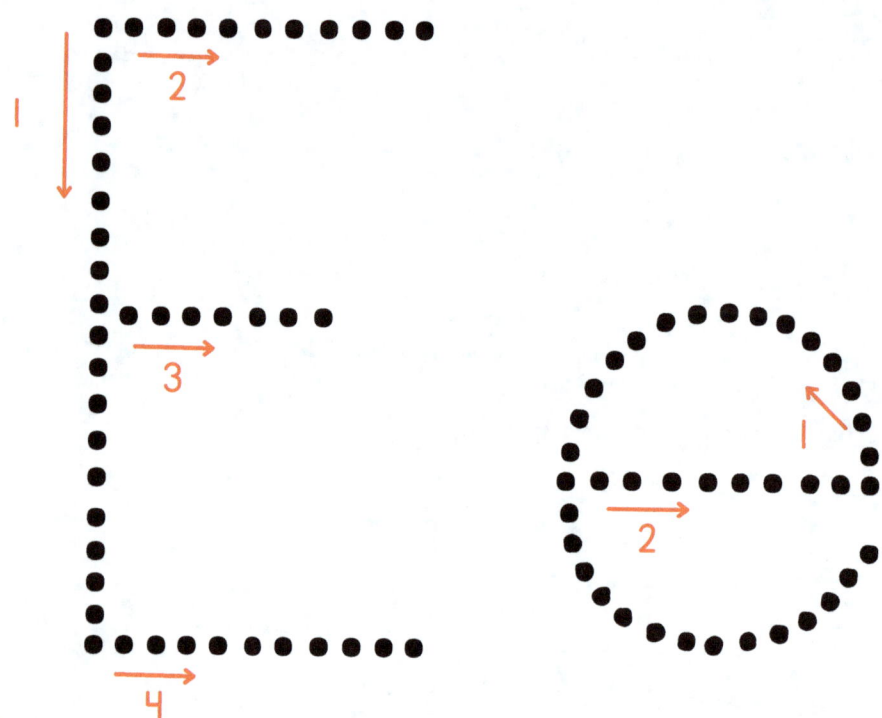

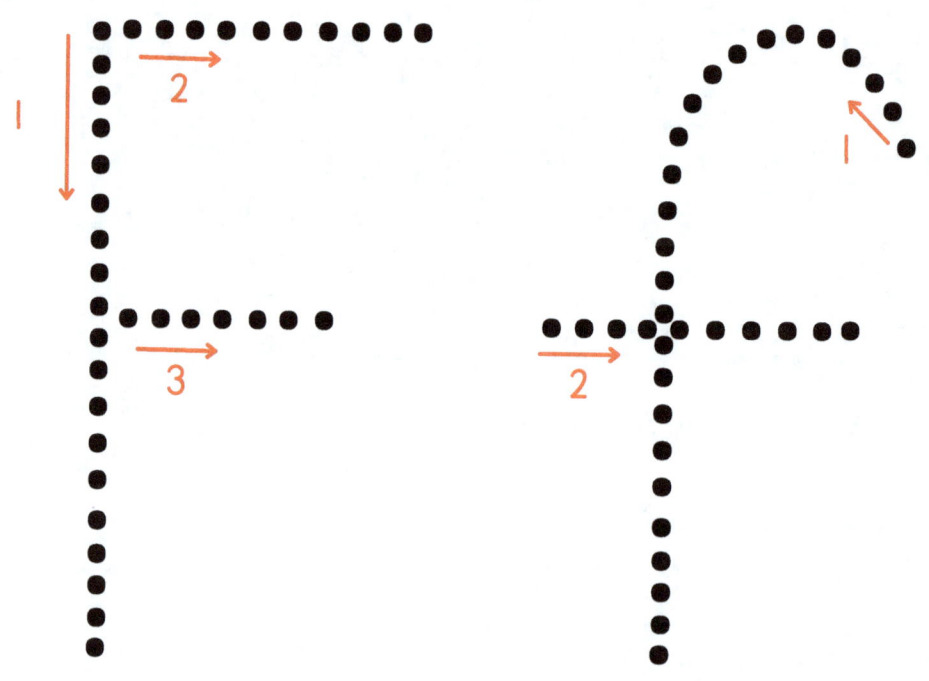

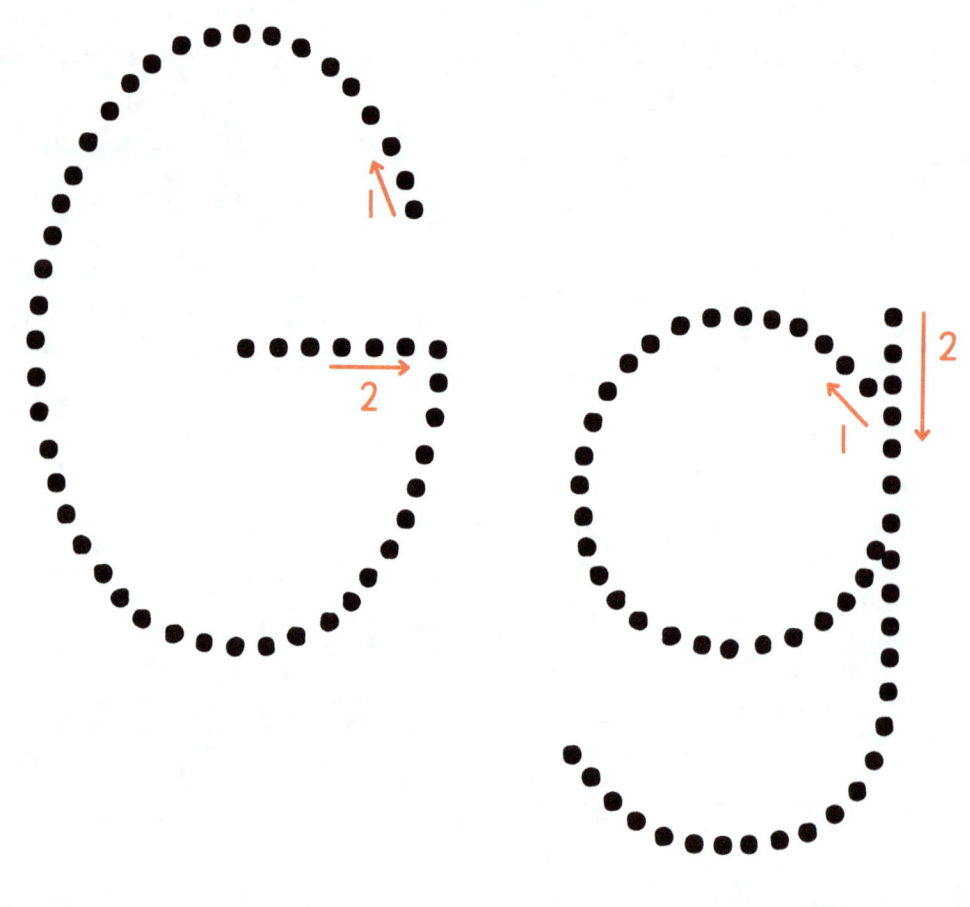

G

g

G

g

G g G g G g G g

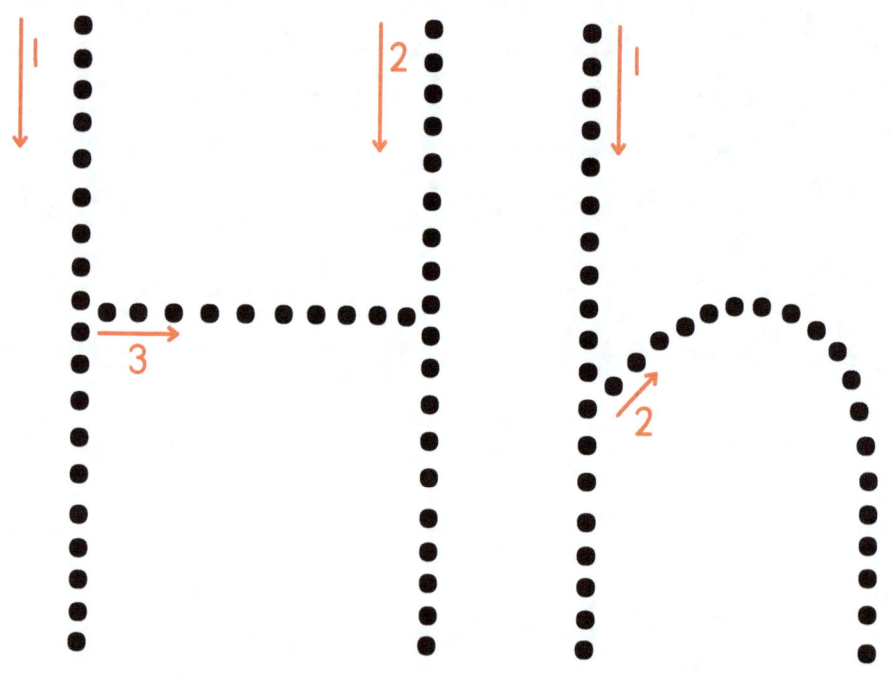

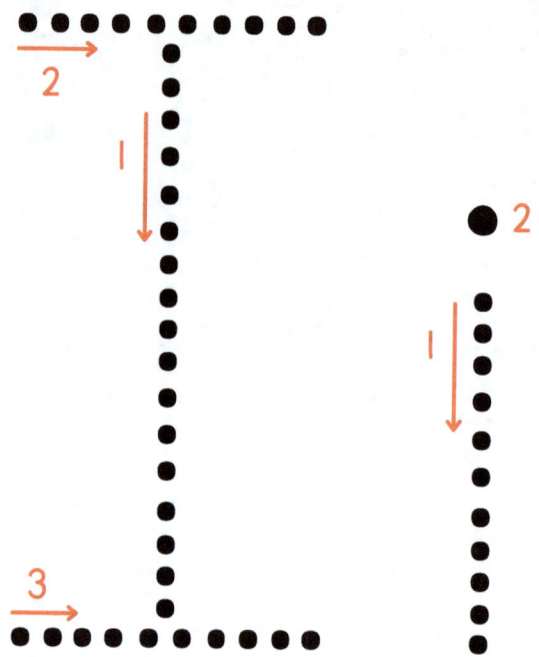

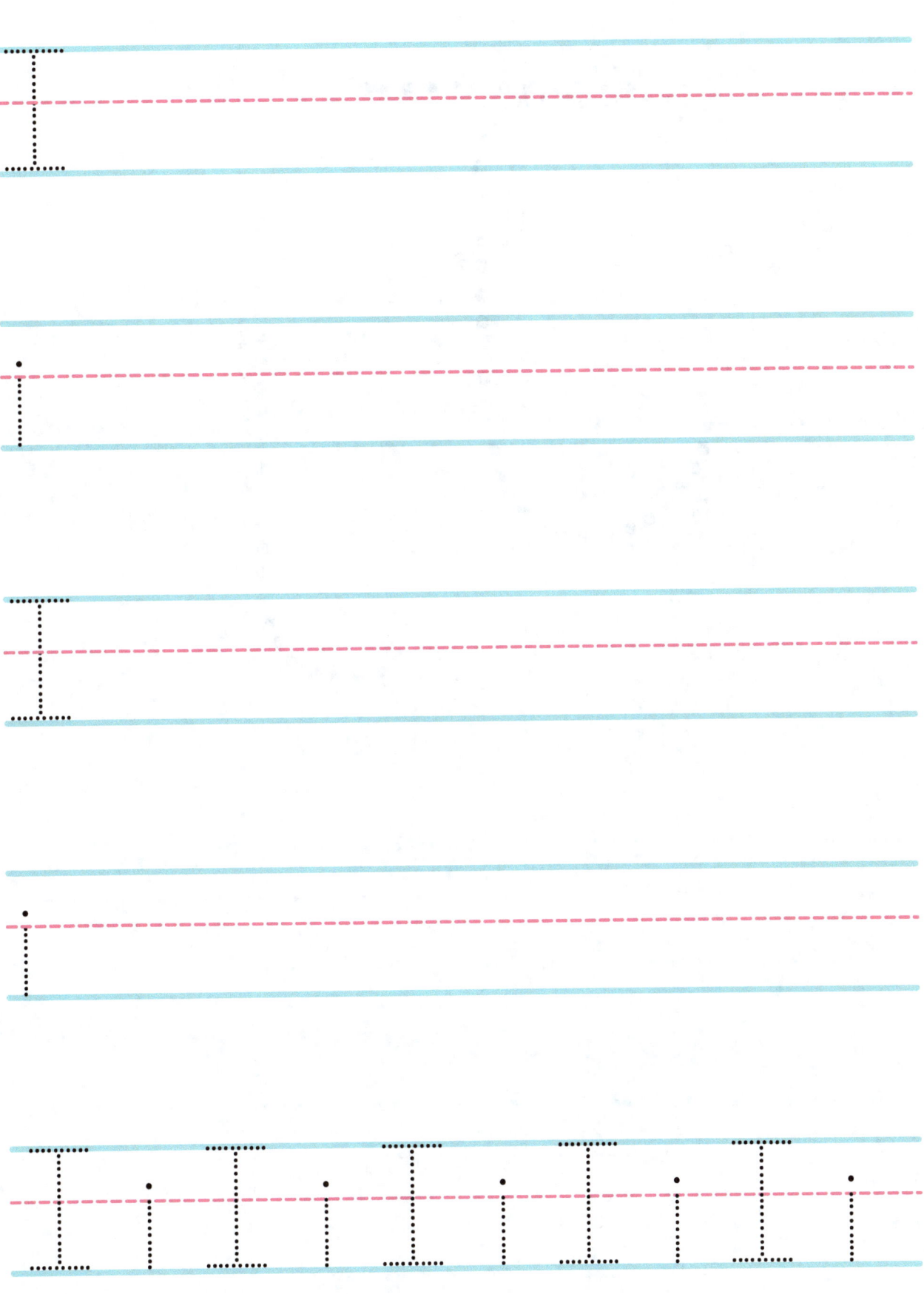

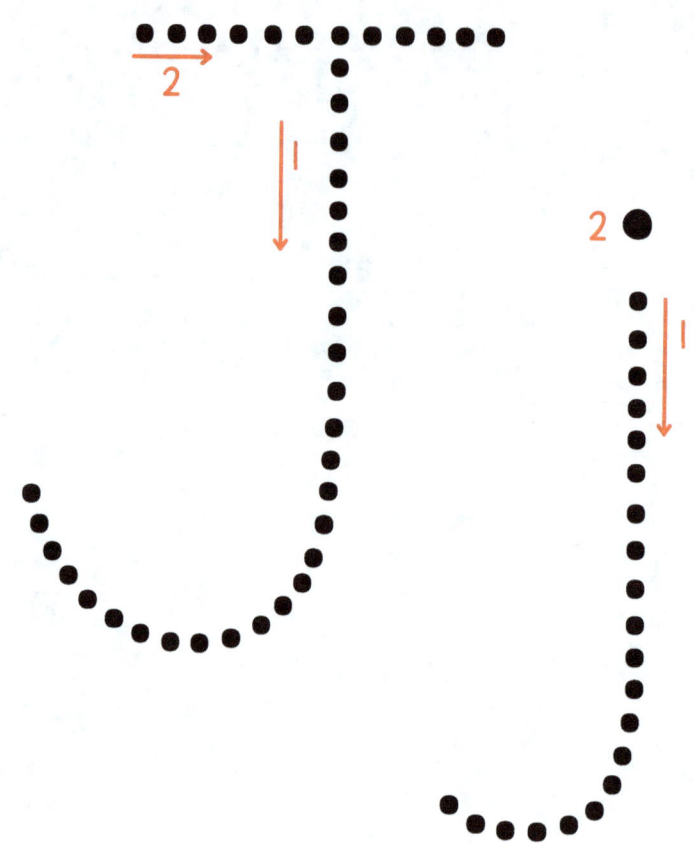

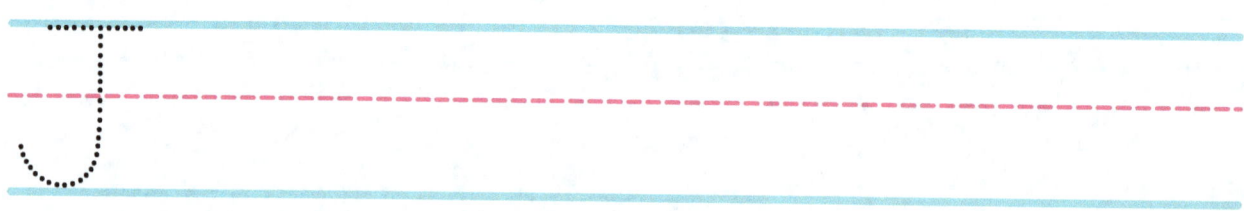

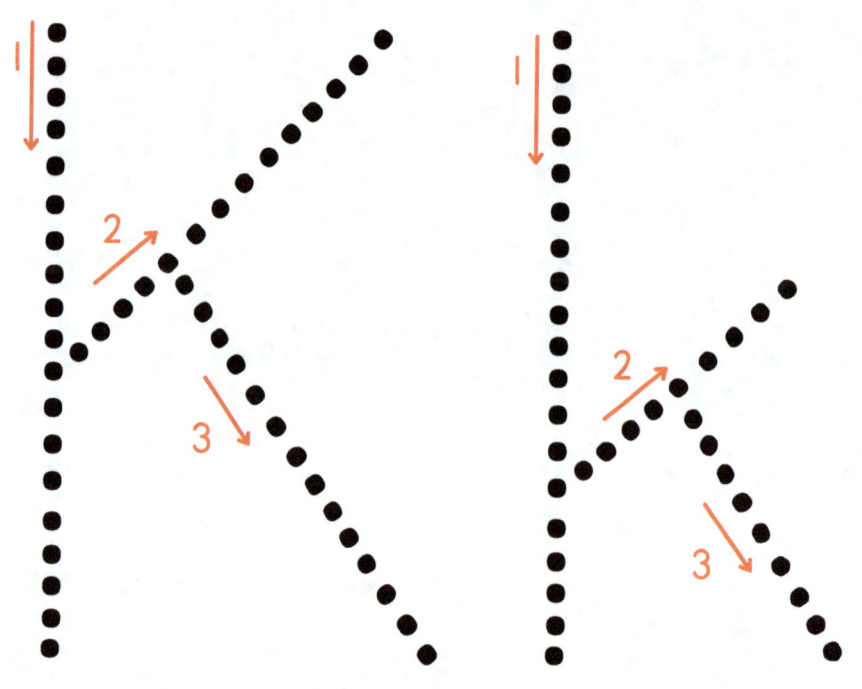

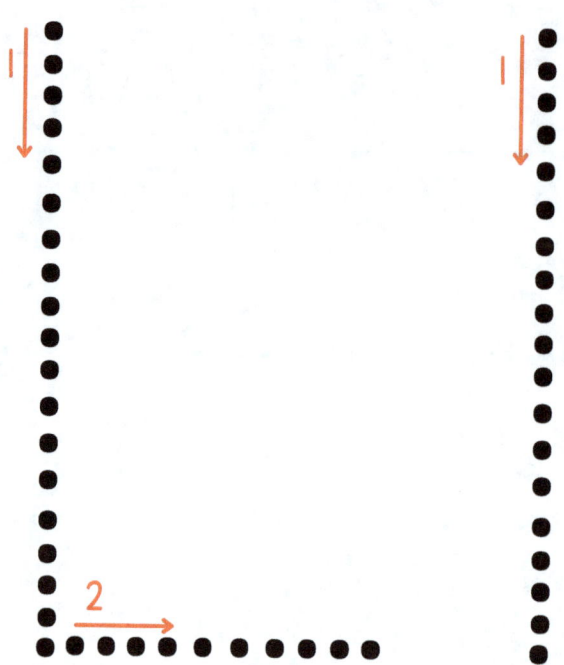

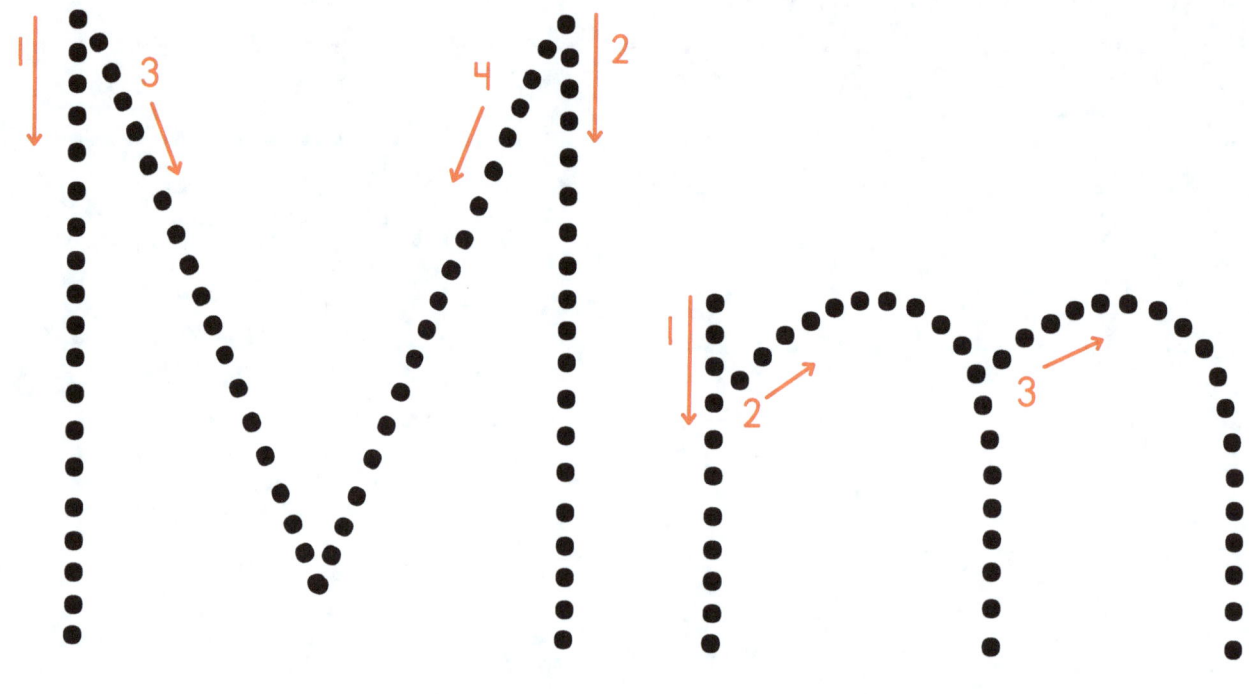

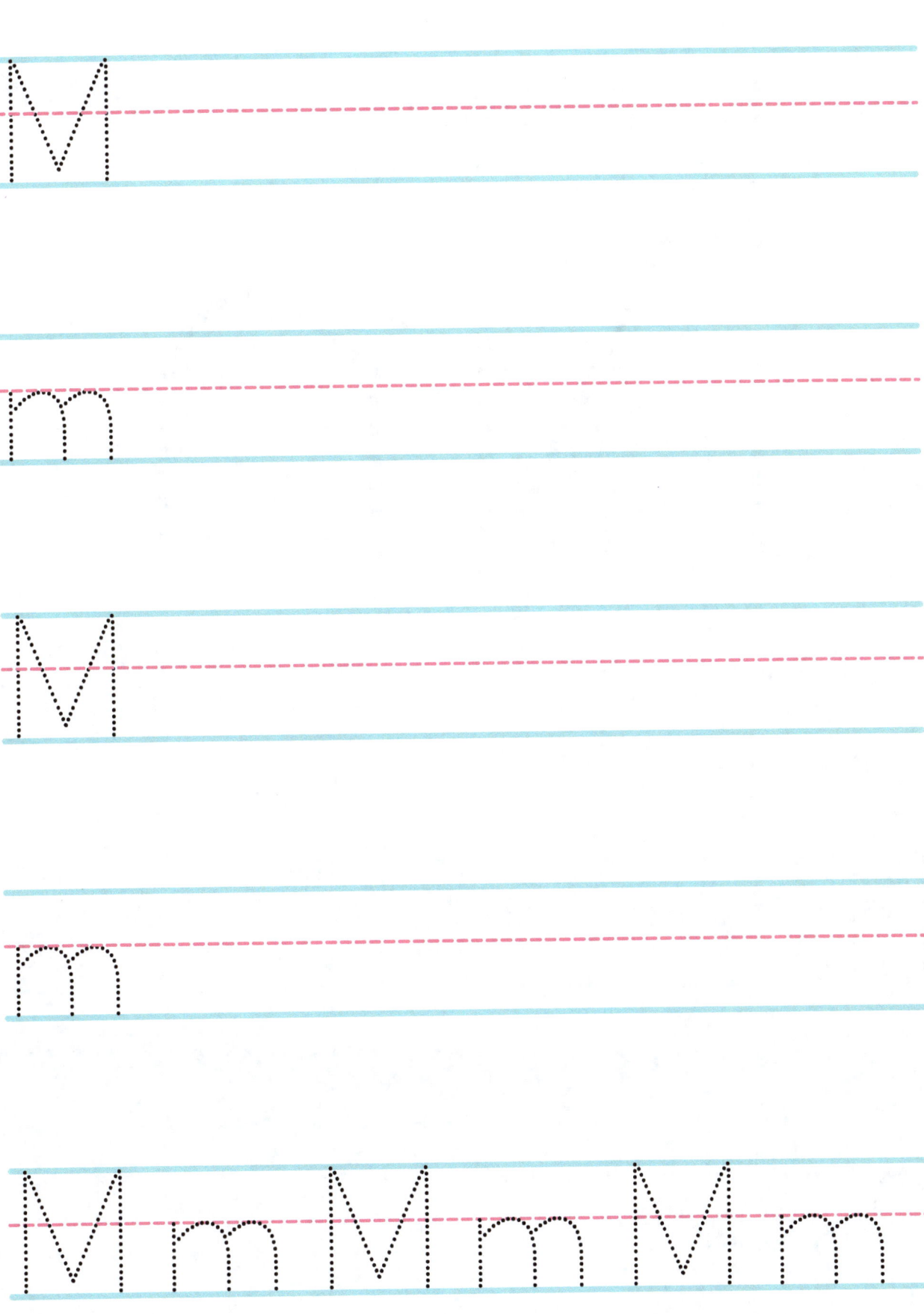

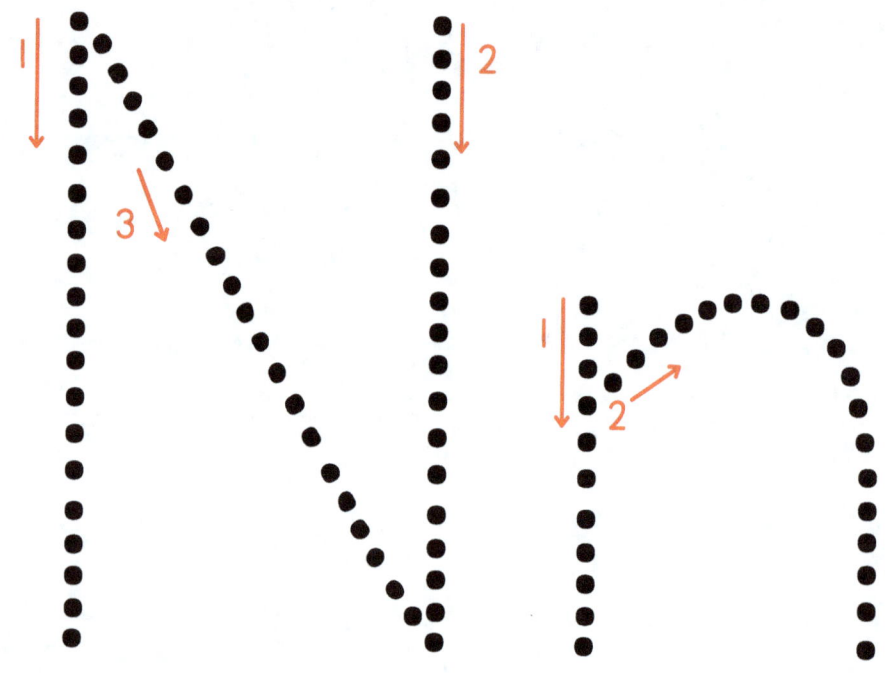

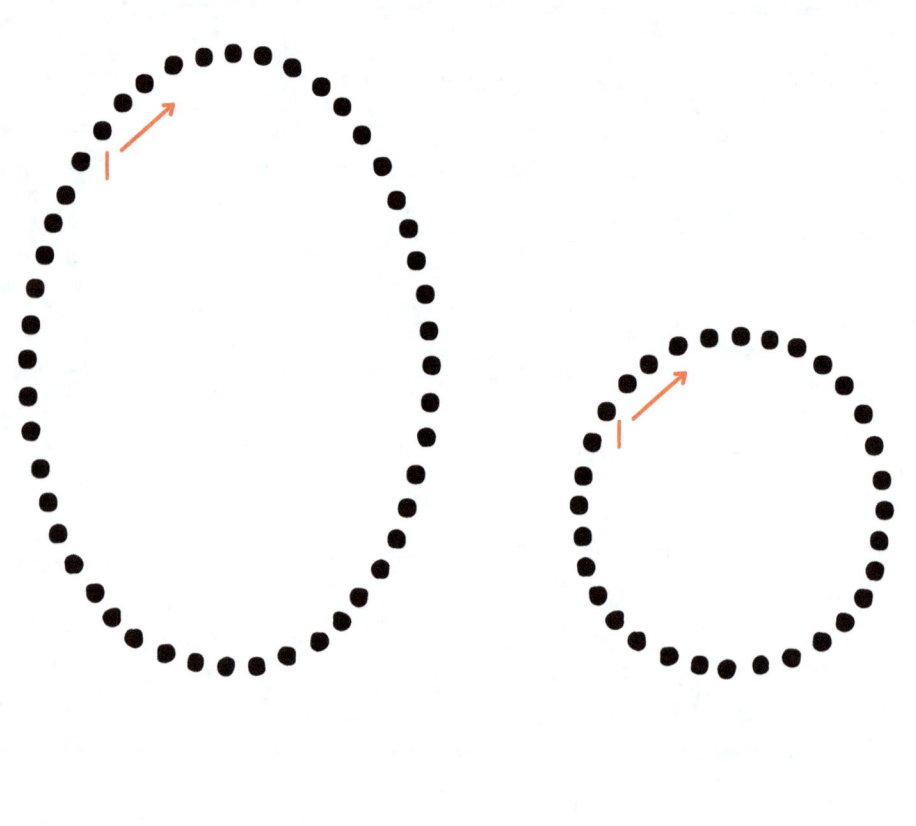

O

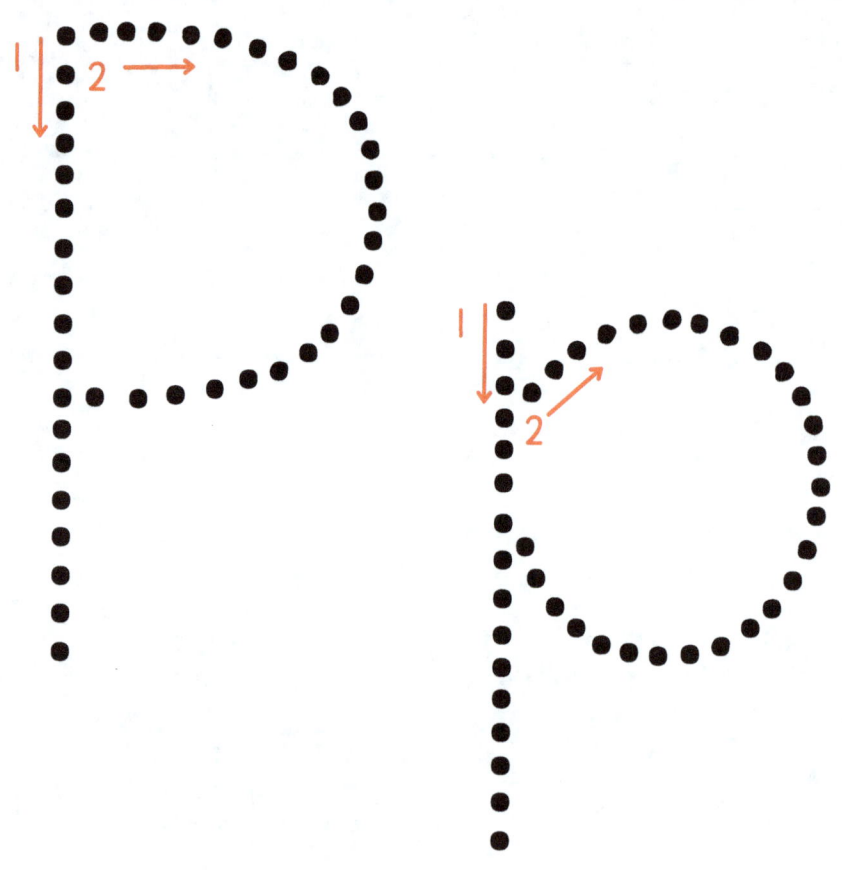

P

p

P

p

P p P p P p P p

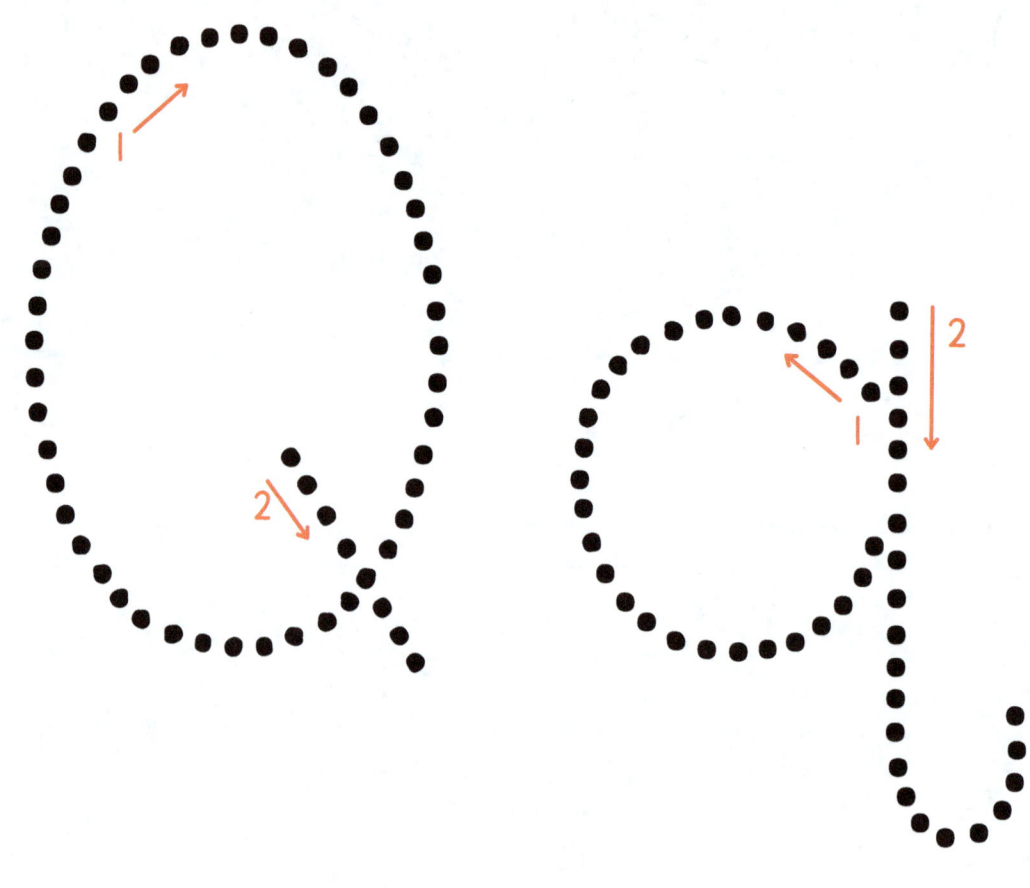

Q

q

Q

q

QqQqQqQqQqQq

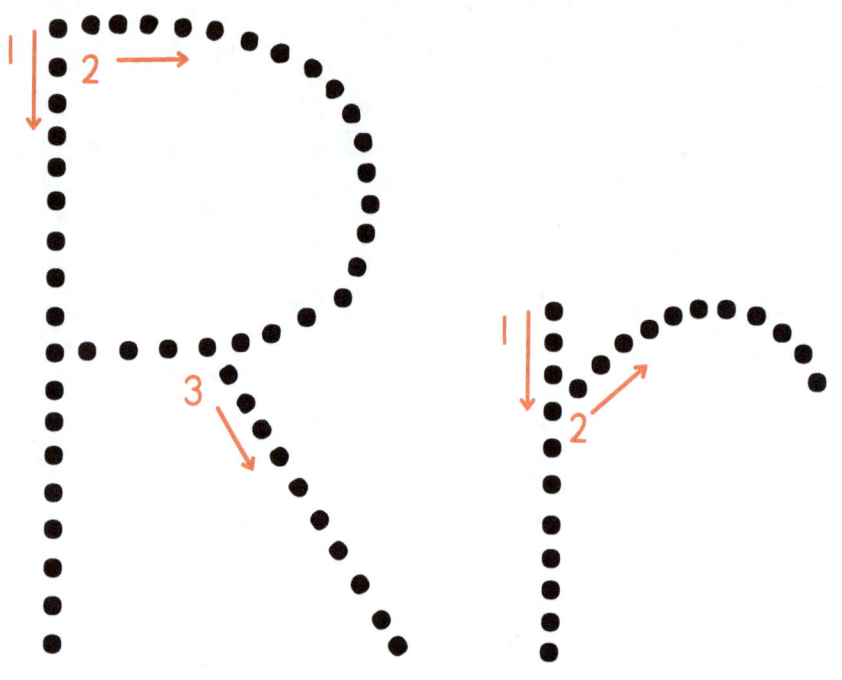

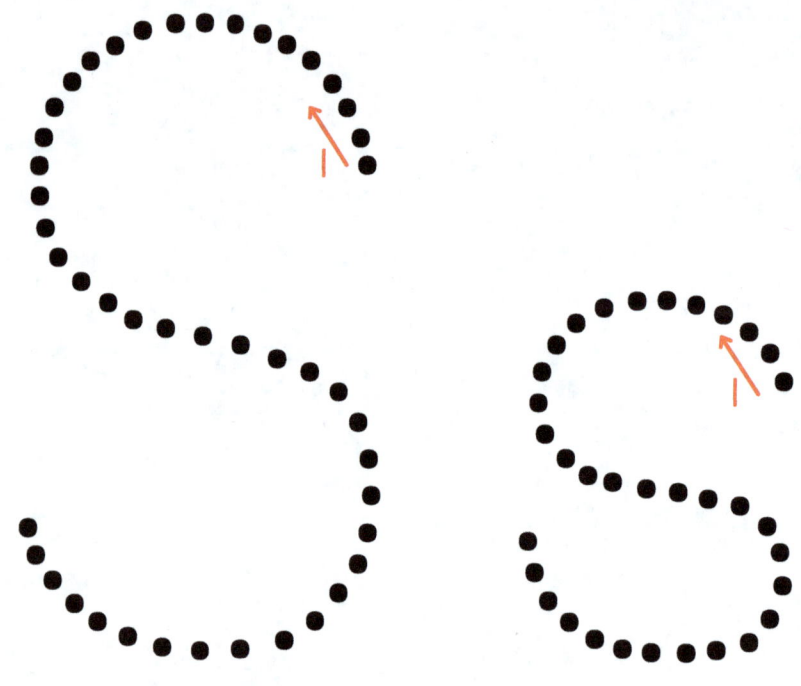

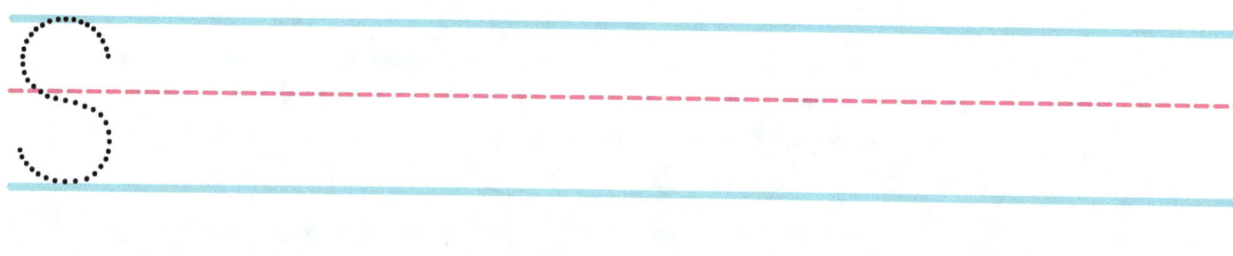

S

s

S

s

S s S s S s S s

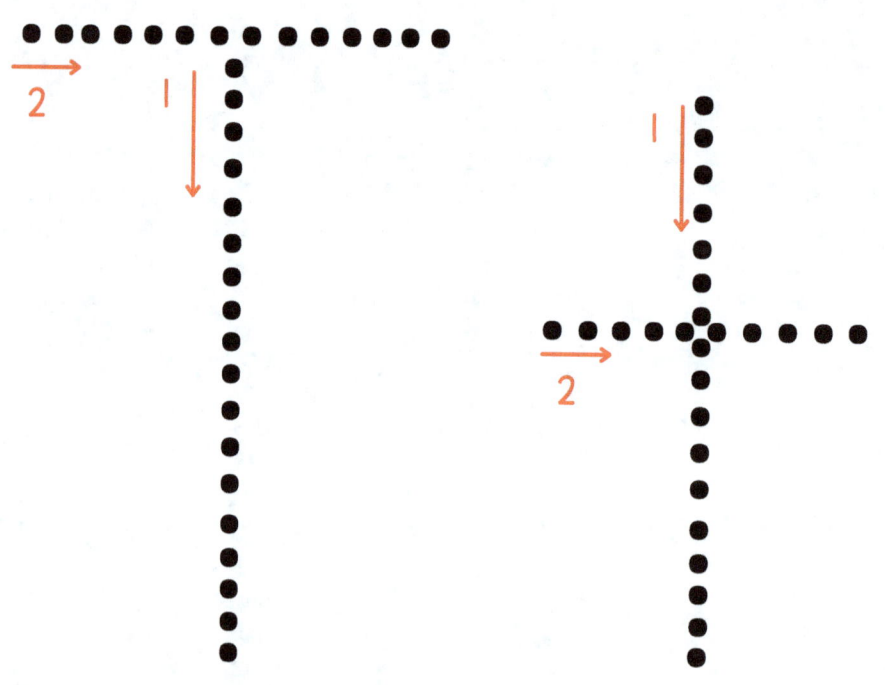

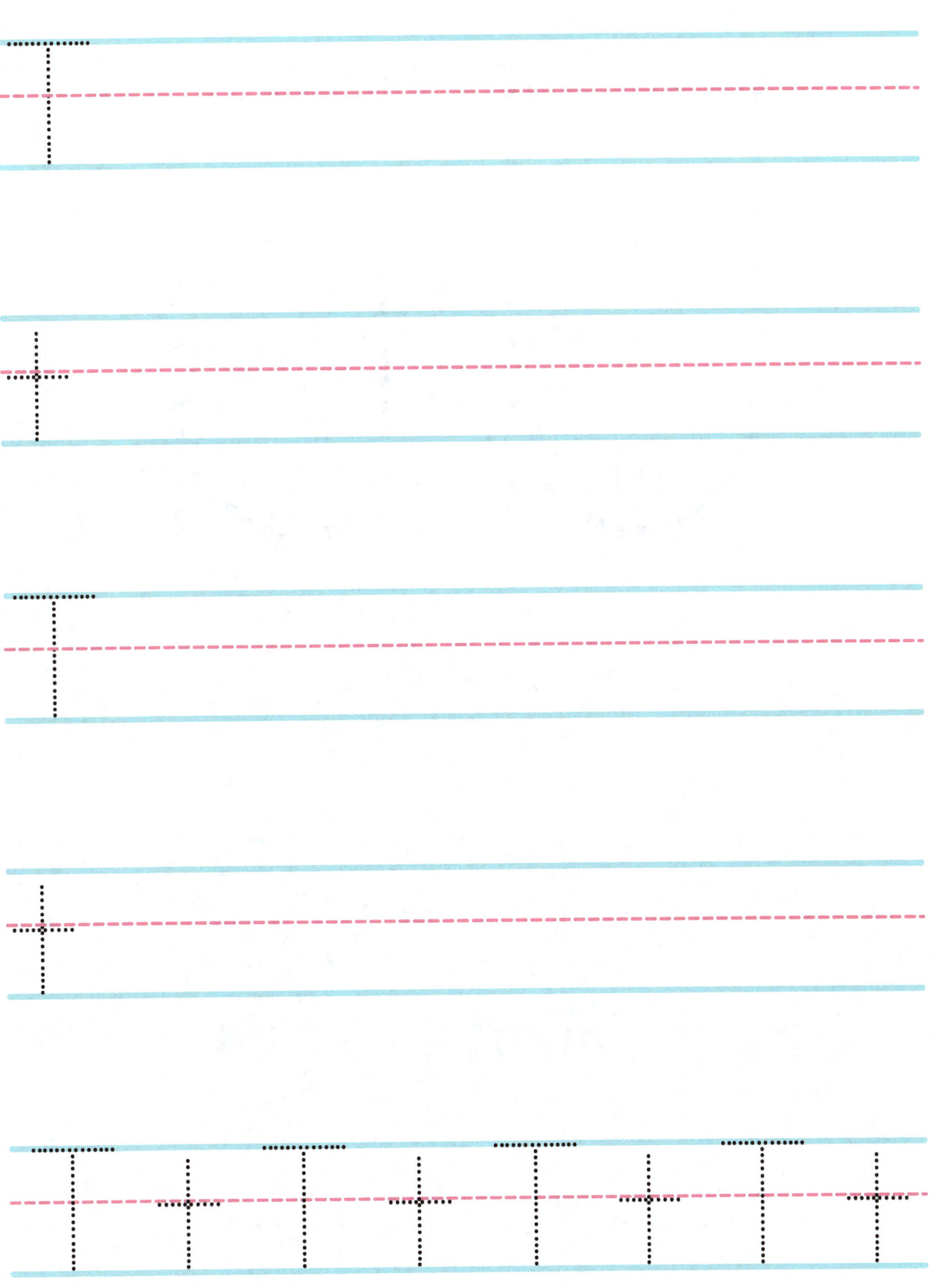

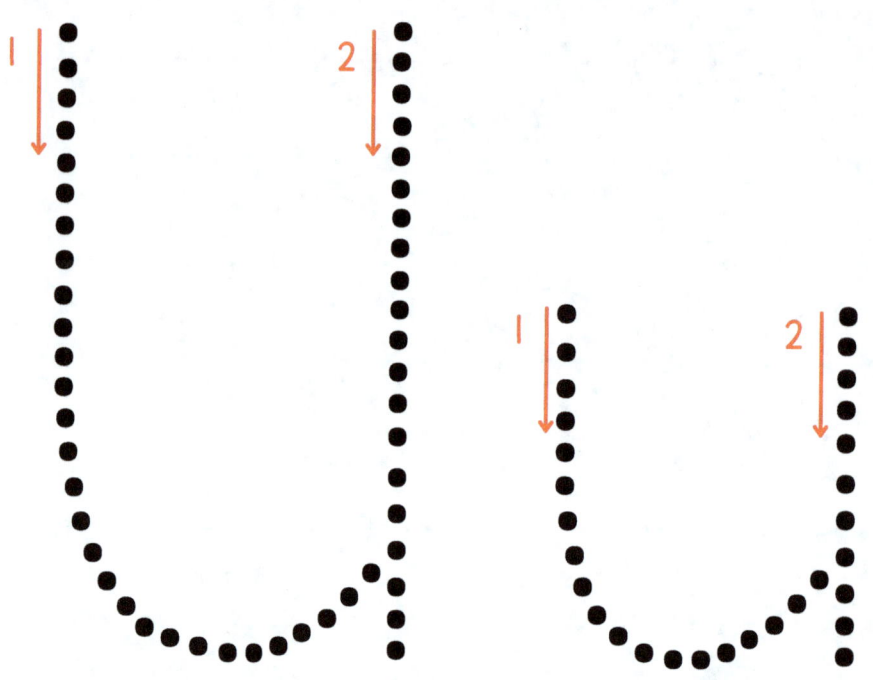

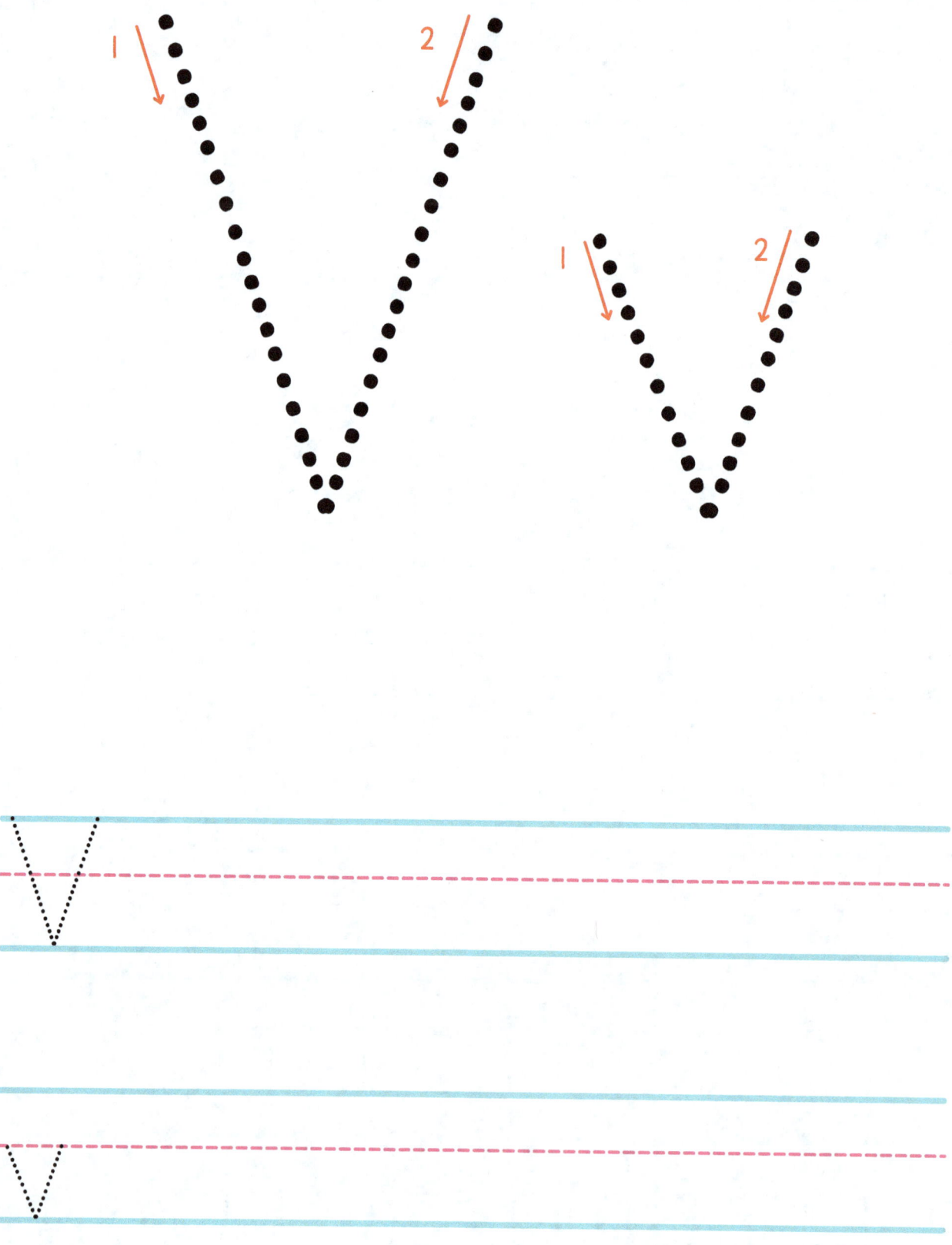

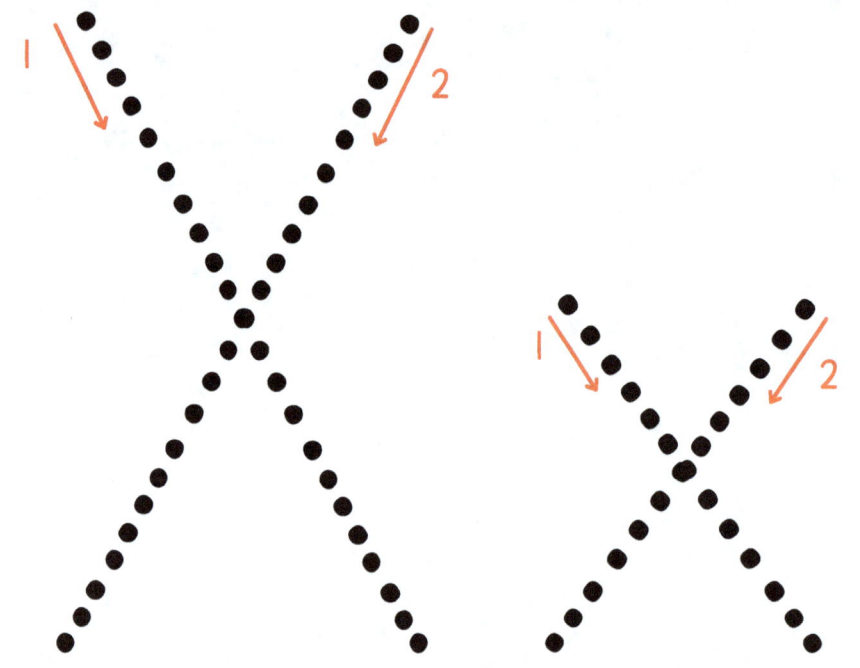

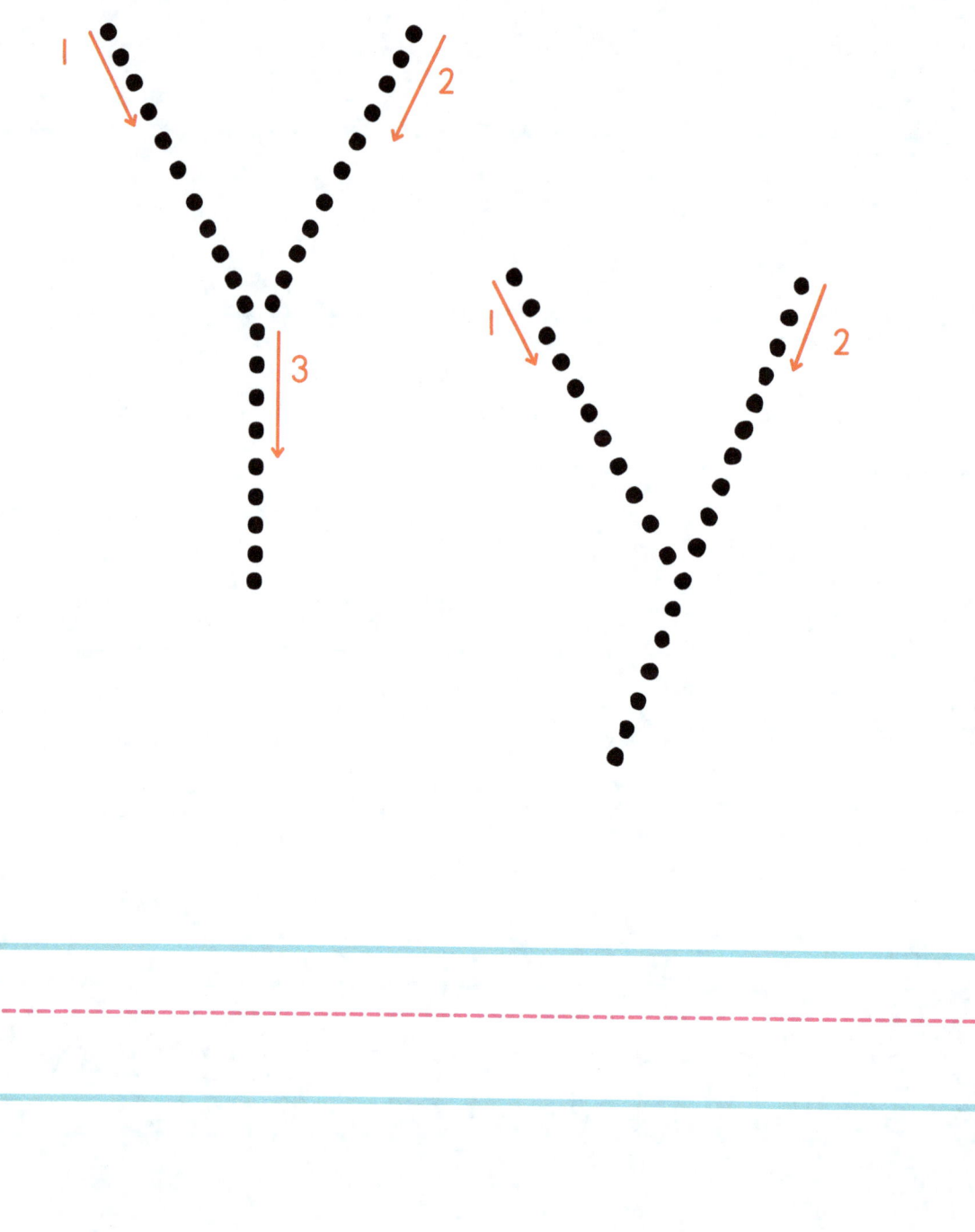

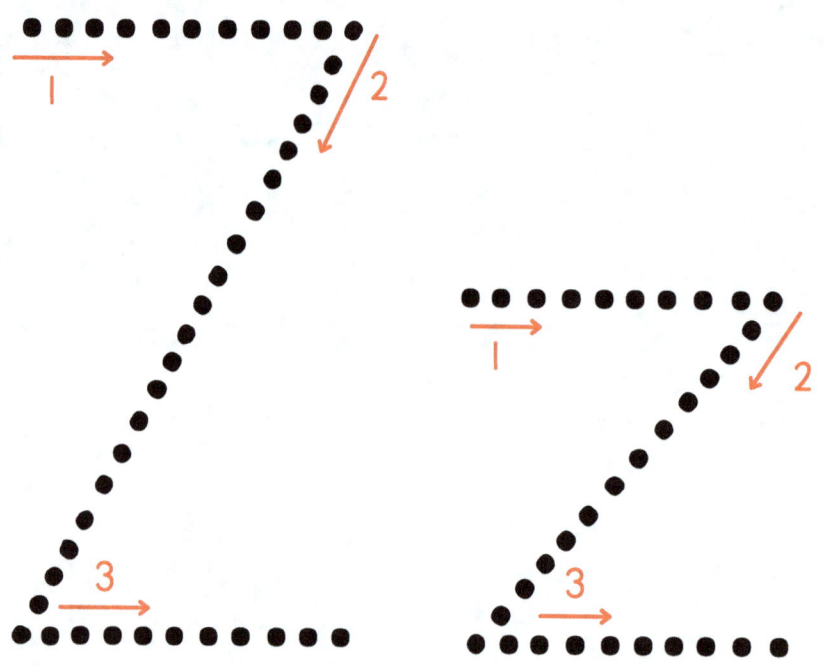

DAYS OF THE WEEK

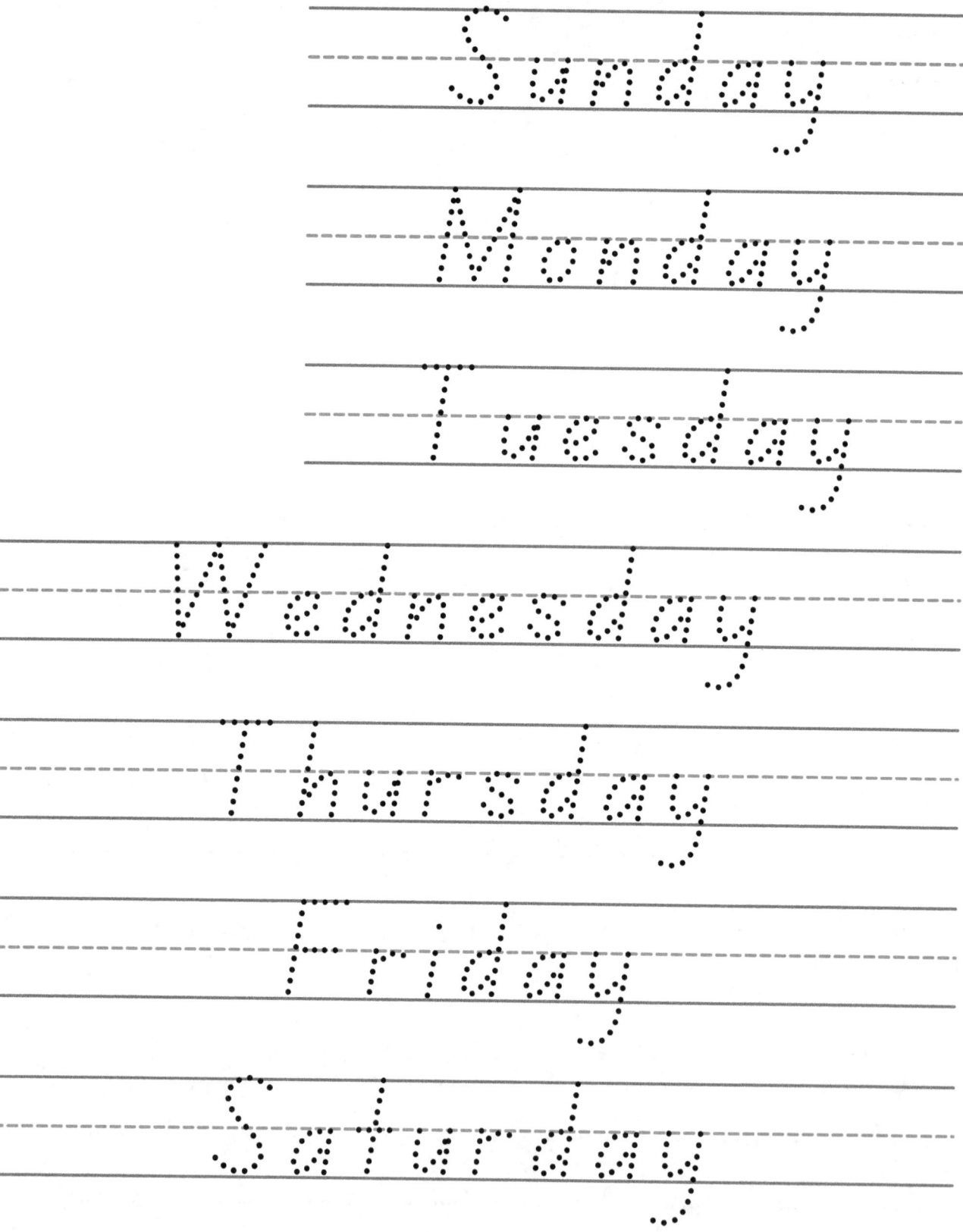

A a

A   A

a   a

Anna is an amazing ant.

B b

B B

b b

Look at the busy bee.

C c

C C

c c

Carl is a colorful cow.

D d

D   D

d   d

Here is a dragonfly.

E e

E E

e e

Here is an elephant.

F f

F F

f f

This frog is funny.

Gg

G G

g g

The gorilla likes grapes.

H h

H H

h h

Henry hippo is huge.

Ii

l   l

i   i

Izzy iguana eats insects.

J j

J j

j j

I see a joyful jellyfish.

K k

K K

k k

Kevin the koala is kind.

L l

L L

l l

Leon the lion loves lollies.

Mm

M M

m m

Mel is a cheeky monkey.

N n

N   N

n   n

Newt play at night.

O o

O O

o o

Oscar is a brown otter.

P p

P P

p p

Pearl is a pretty panda.

Q q

Q Q

q q

Quokkas are quiet.

R r

R R

r r

The rooster rocks on!

S s

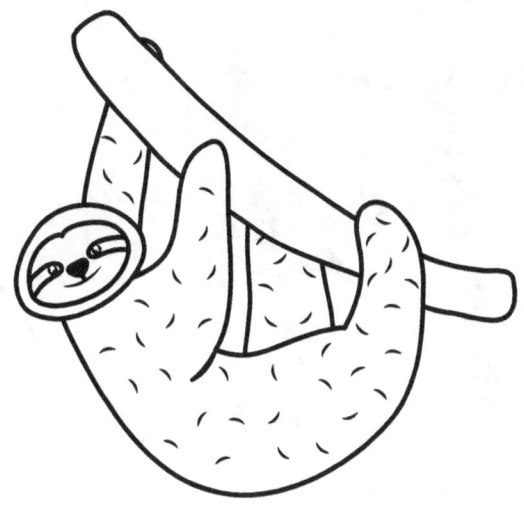

S S

s s

Sally sloth sleeps a lot.

T t

T T

t t

Terry is a tired turtle.

U u

U U

u u

Unicorns are unique.

V v

V V

v v

Vultures are very big!

W W

w w

Whales swim in water.

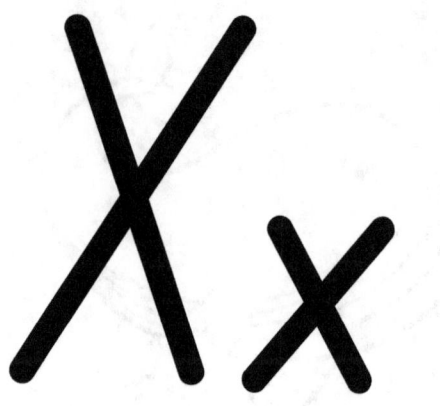
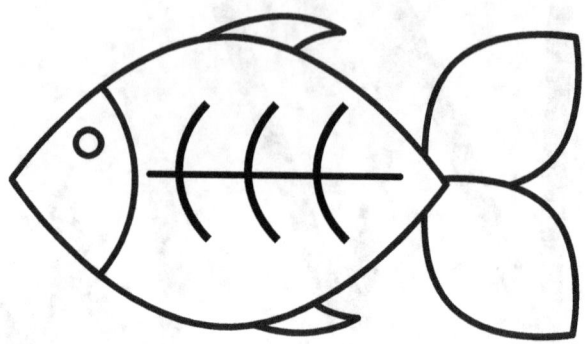

X x

x x

This is an x-ray fish.

Y y

y y

y y

The yak is funny.

Zz

Z Z

z z

Zoe the zebra zig zags.

MONTHS OF THE YEAR

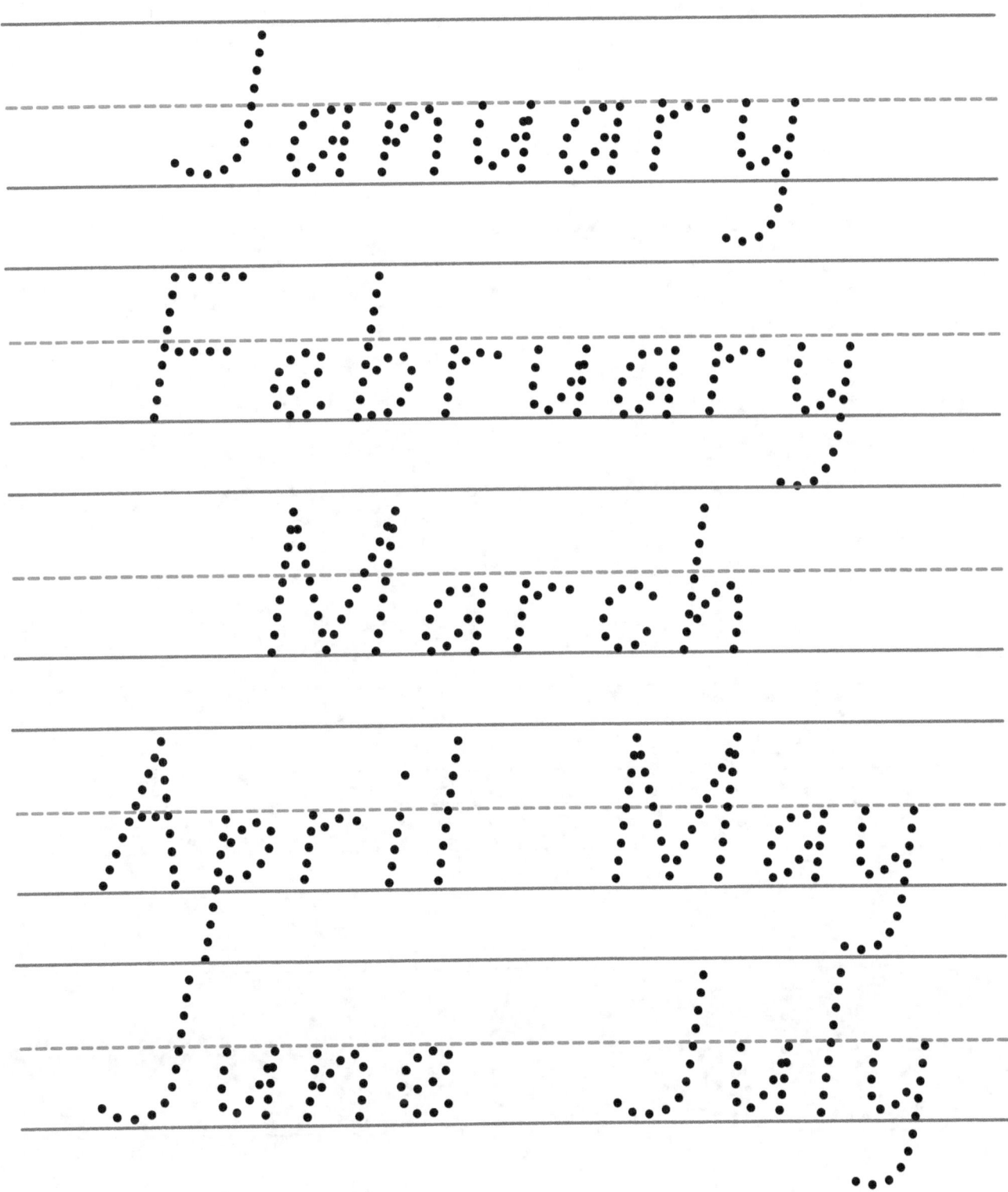

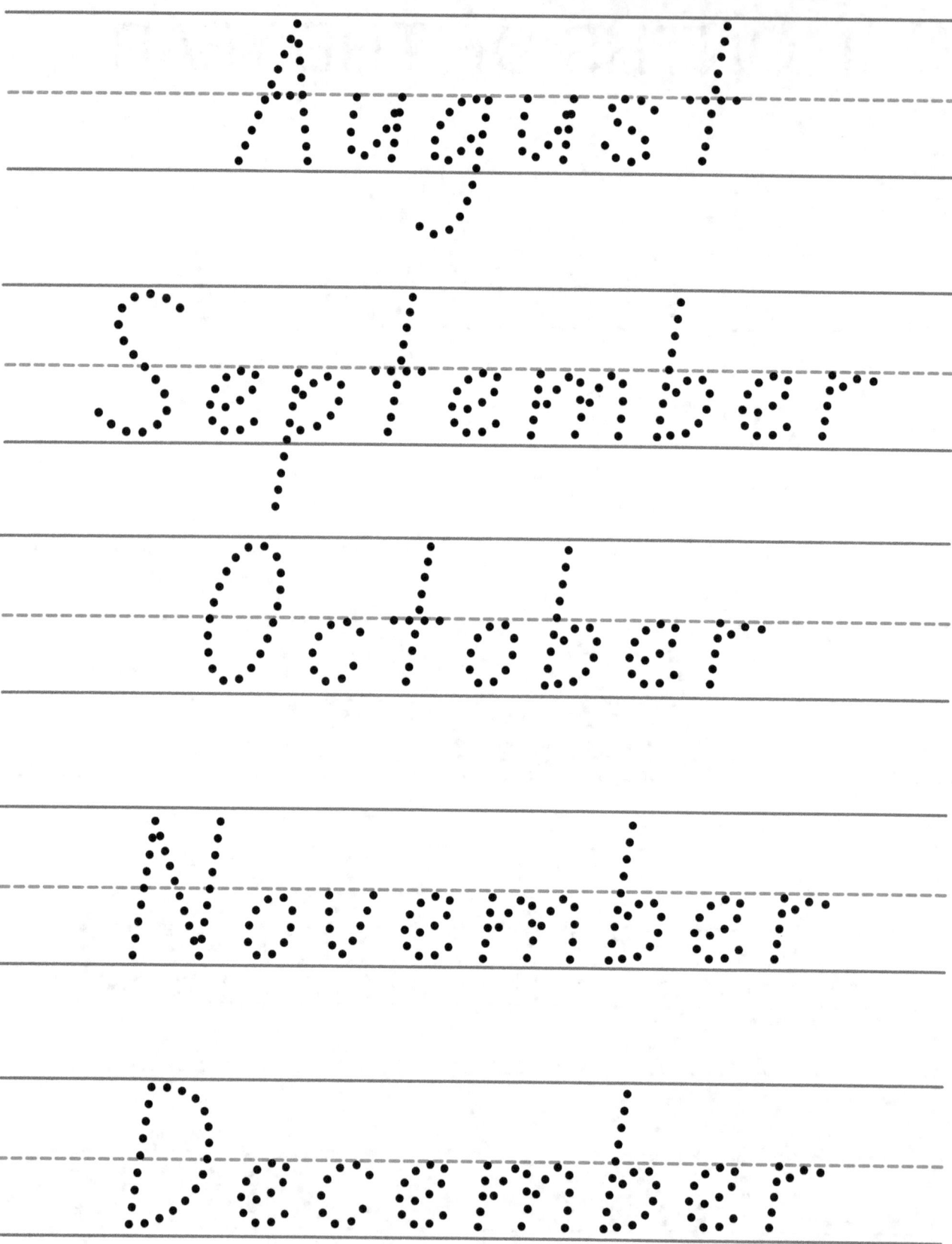

ABOUT MY COMMUNITY

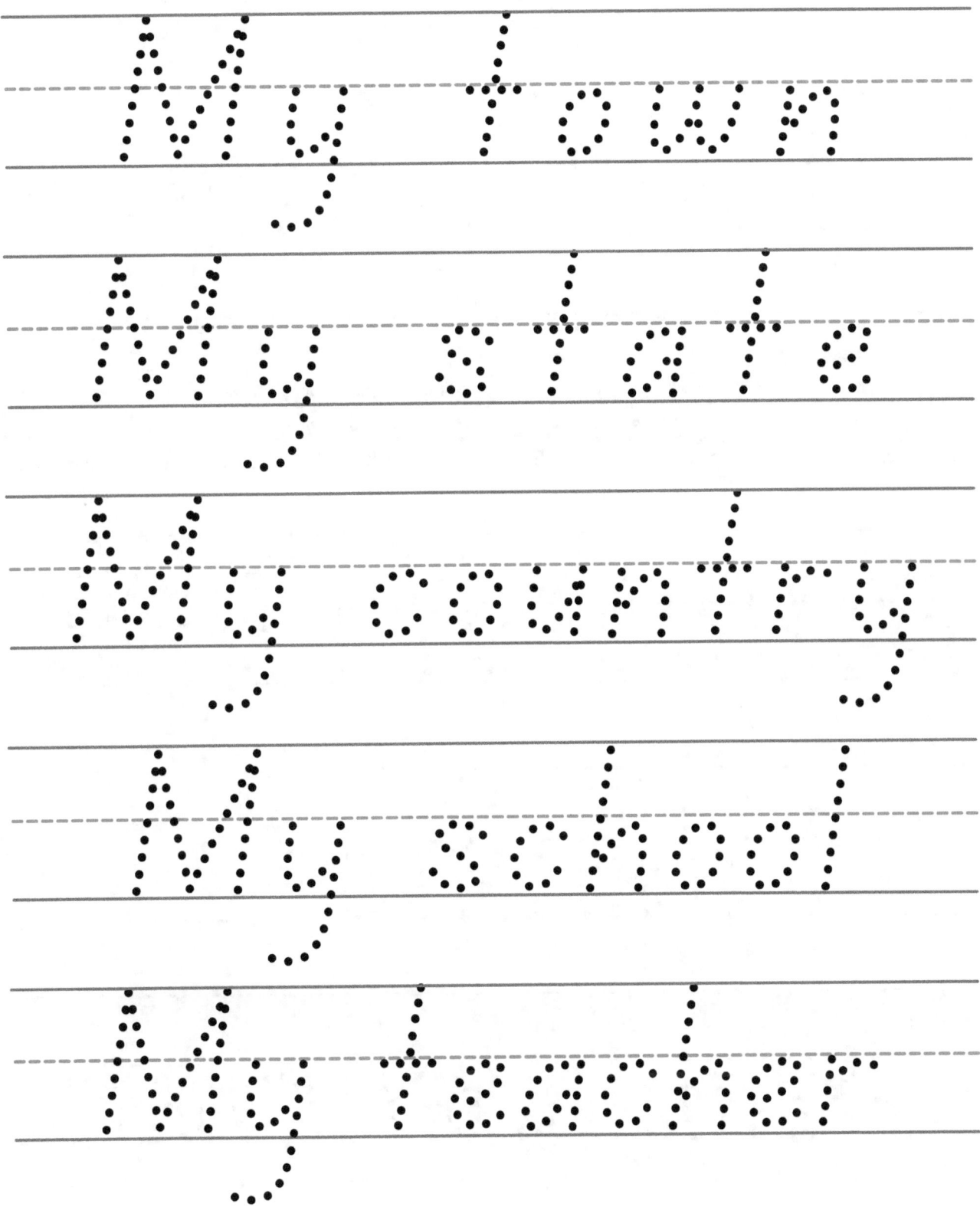

My town

My state

My country

My school

My teacher

WORKERS IN COMMUNITY

firefighter

doctor

police officer

dentist

mail carrier

FROM ZERO TO TEN

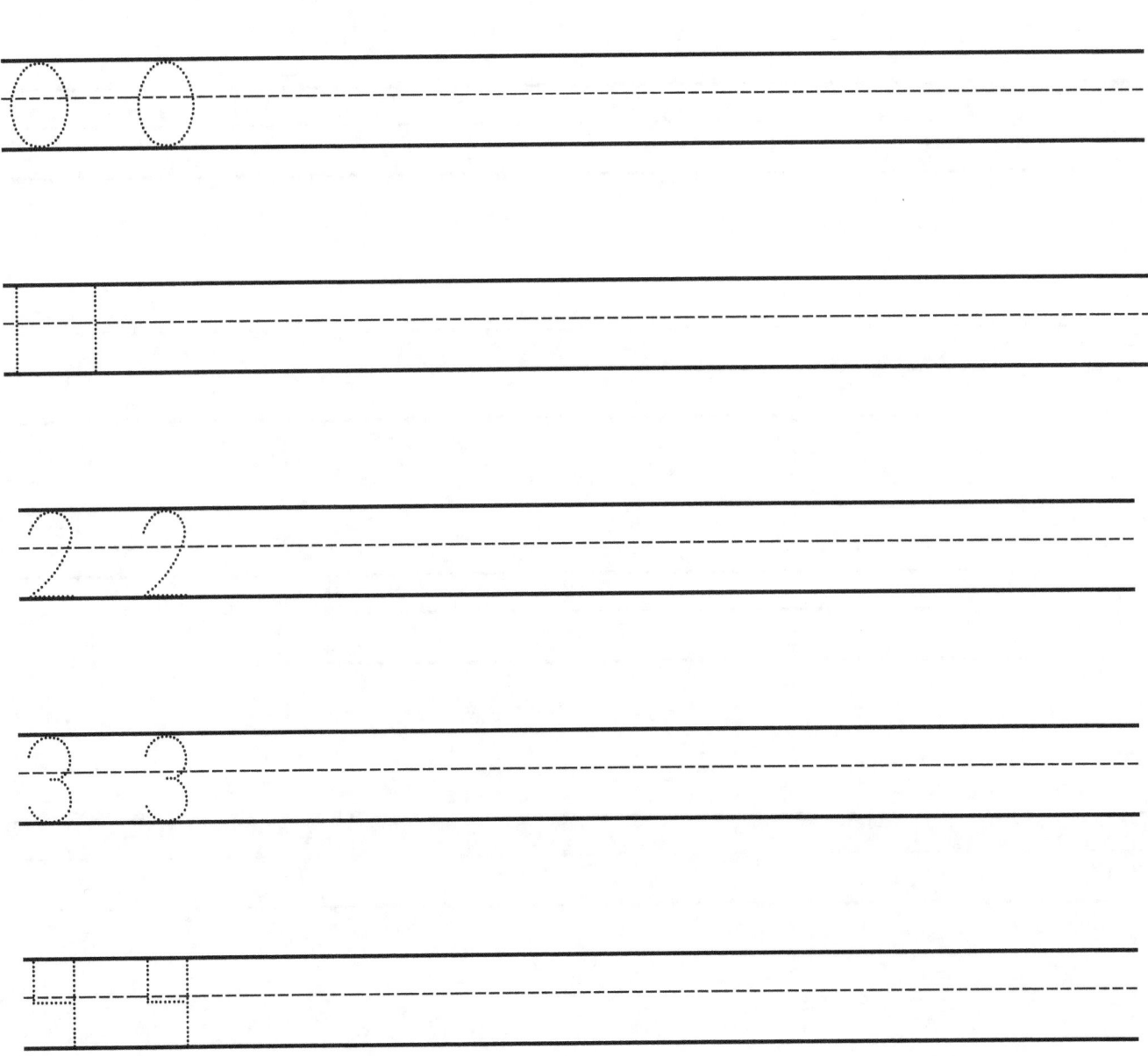

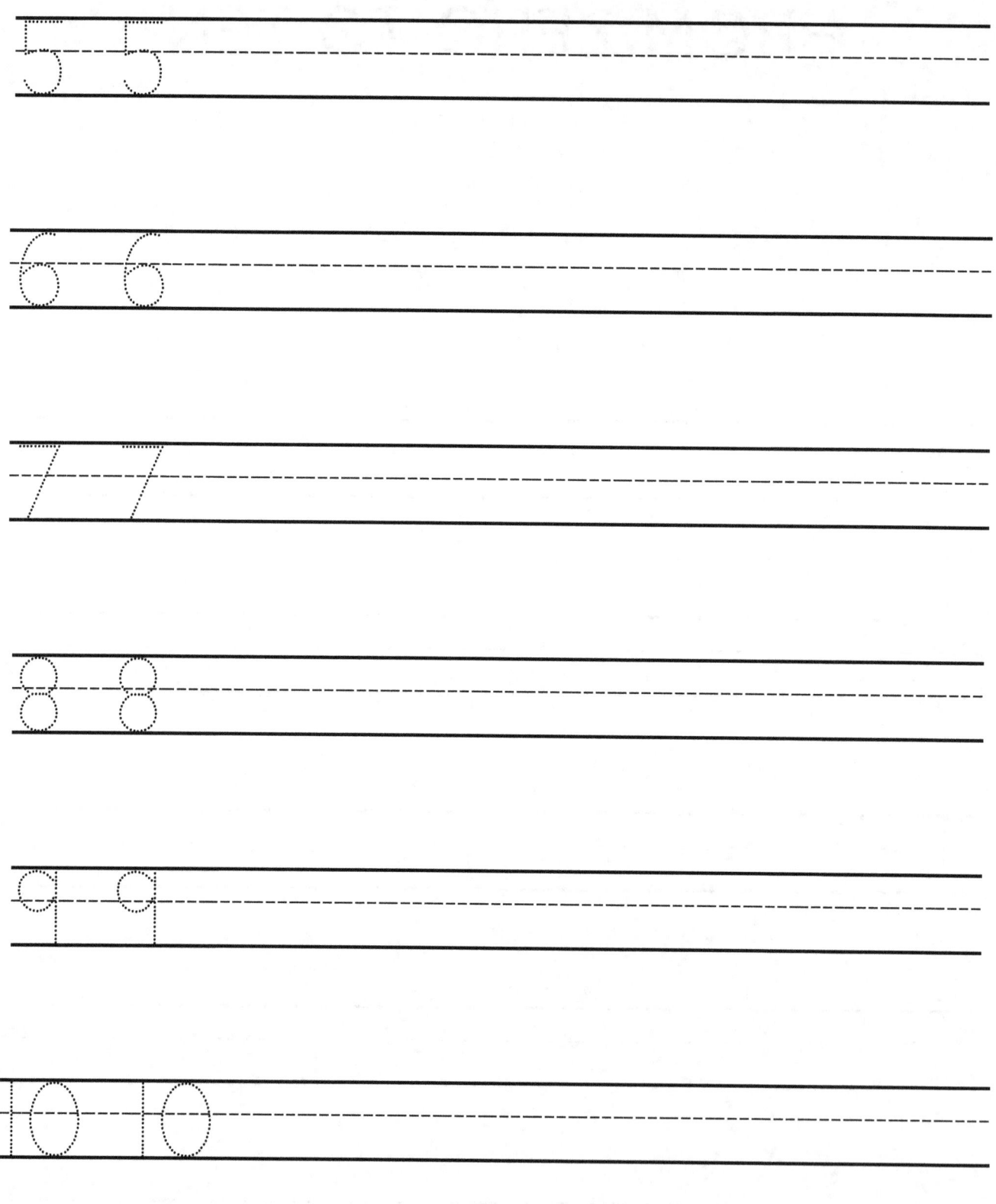

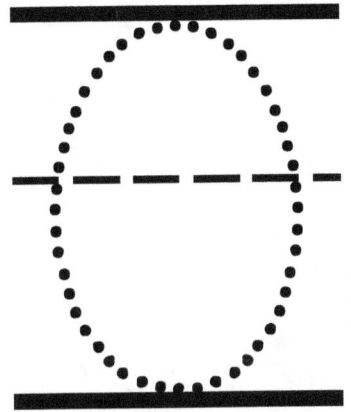

zero

I one

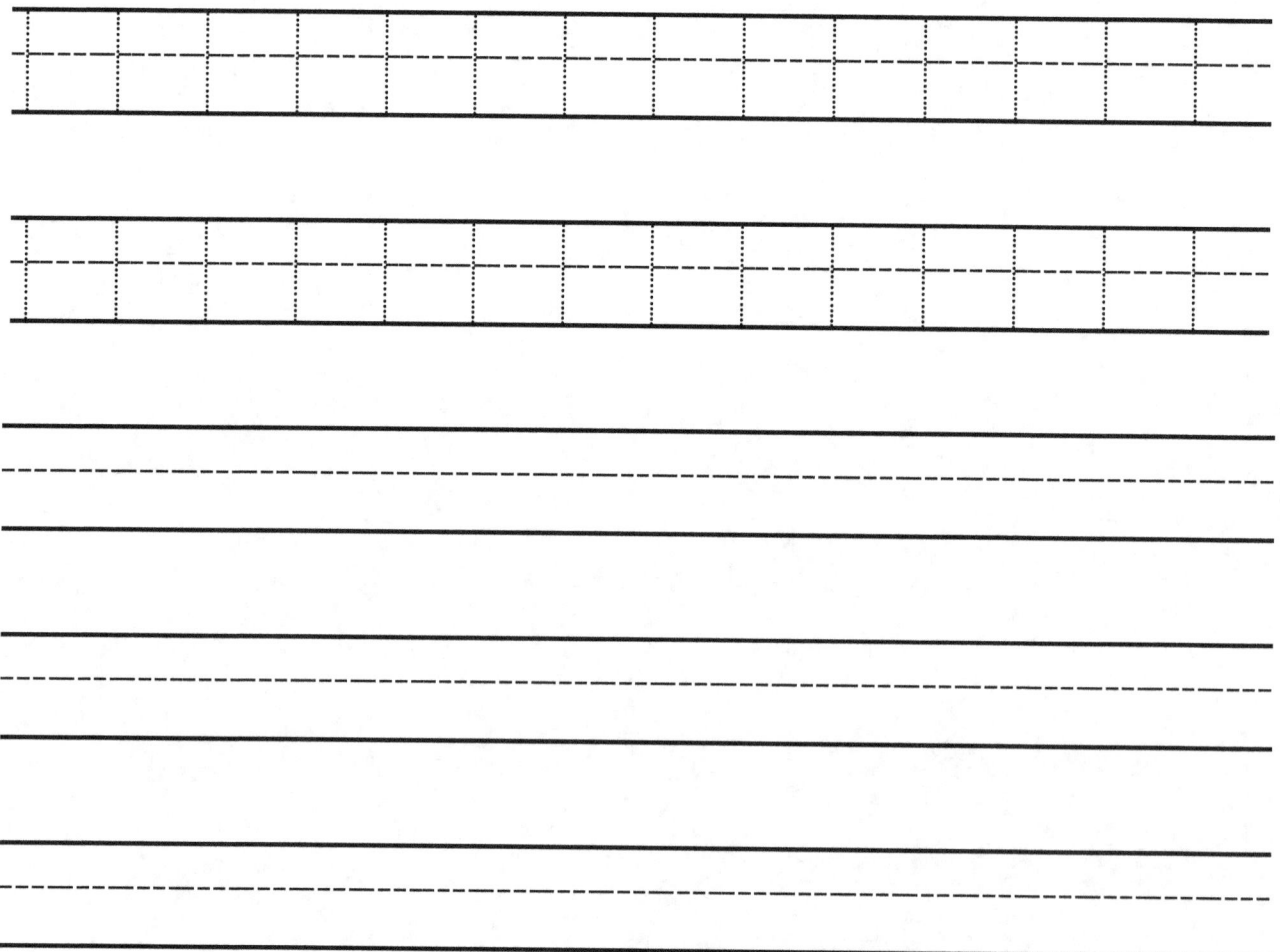

2

two

2 2 2 2 2 2 2 2 2 2

2 2 2 2 2 2 2 2 2 2

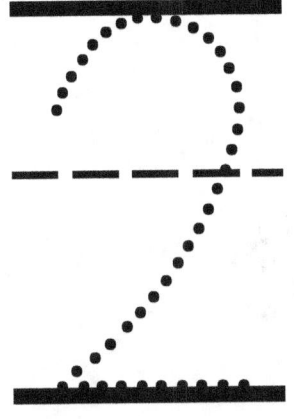

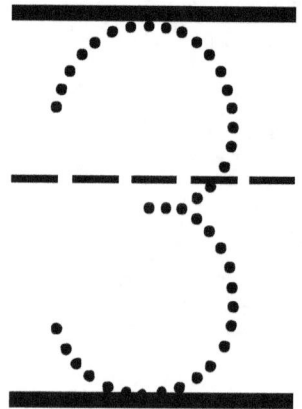

three

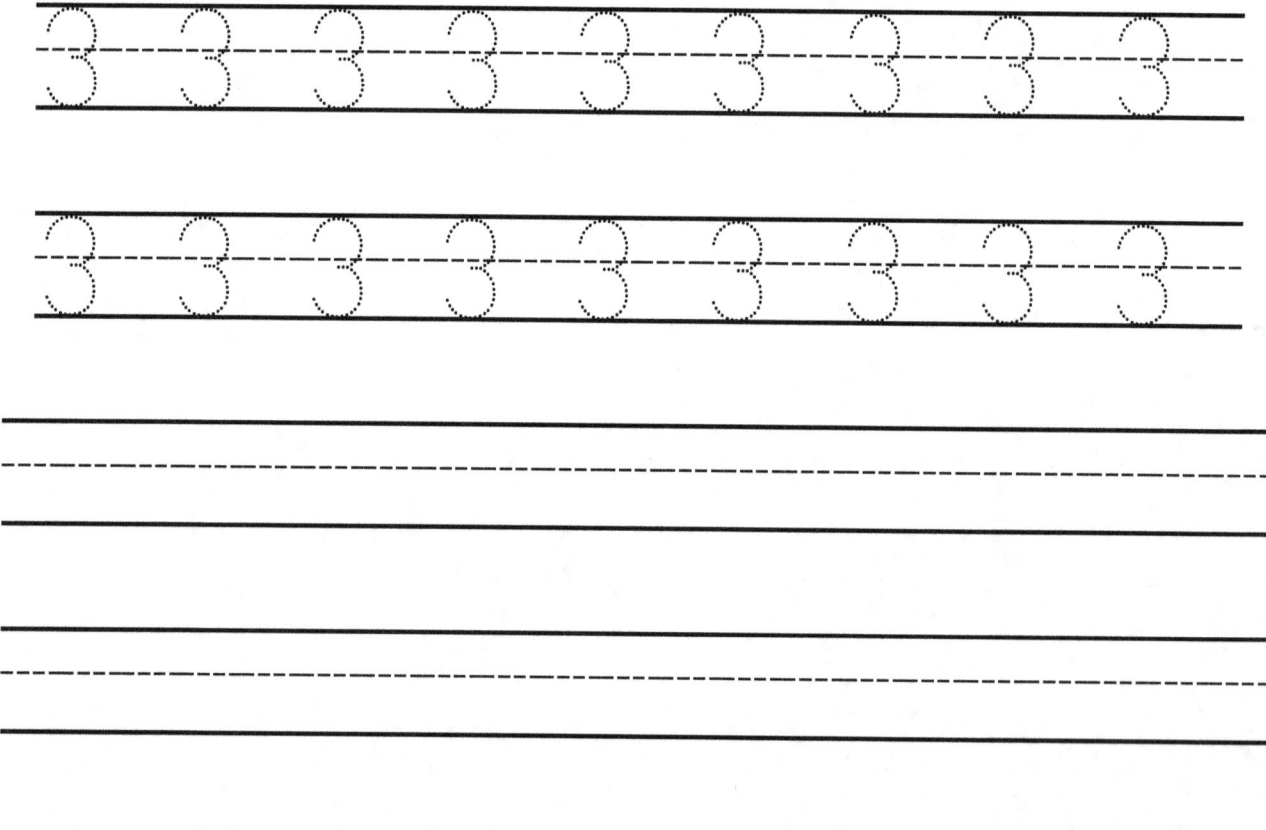

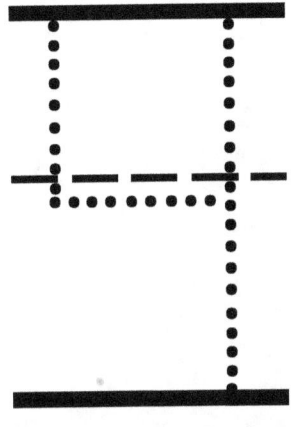

four

5 five

5 5 5 5 5 5 5 5 5 5

5 5 5 5 5 5 5 5 5 5

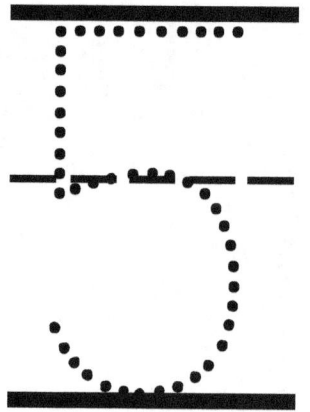

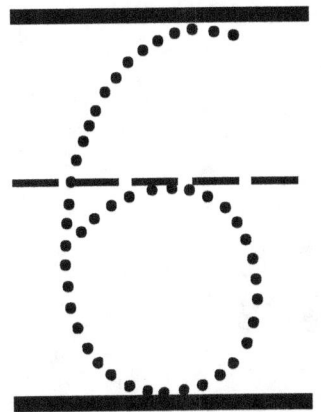

six

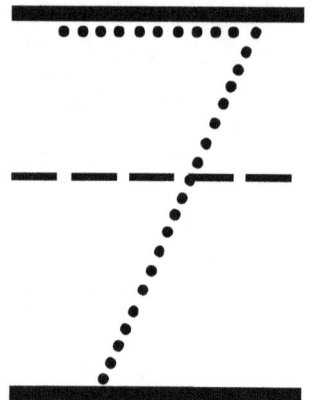

seven

8

eight

8 8 8 8 8 8 8 8 8 8

8 8 8 8 8 8 8 8 8 8

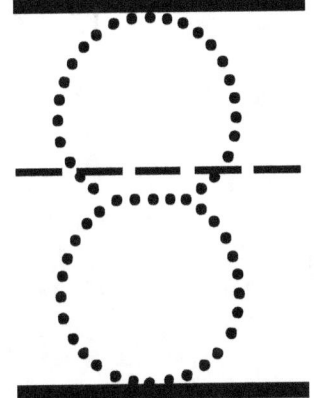

9

nine

9 9 9 9 9 9 9 9 9 9

9 9 9 9 9 9 9 9 9 9

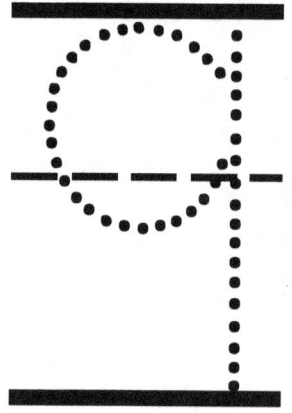

10

ten

10 10 10 10 10 10 10

10 10 10 10 10 10 10

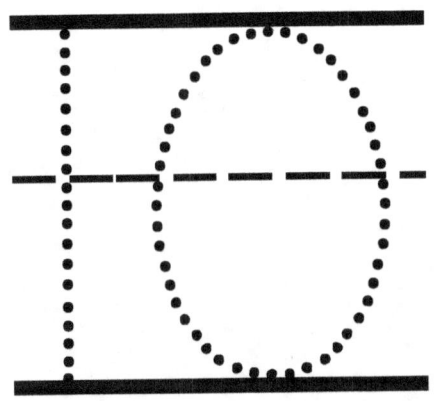

THANKYOU FOR USING THE WORKBOOK